CAPE MAY
A TO Z

Written by
Paige Cunningham & Janet Payne

Illustrated by
the Community of Cape May

CAPE MAY A TO Z

© 2013 BY PAIGE CUNNINGHAM & JANET PAYNE

ART WORK © 2013 BY PAIGE CUNNINGHAM & JANET PAYNE

ISBN 978-1484921166
Library of Congress Control Number: 2013939868

All rights reserved. No part of this book may be reproduced or transmitted in any form or by any means, electronic or mechanical, including photocopying, recording or by any information storage or retrieval system without written permission from the author, except for inclusions of brief quotations in a review.

PUBLICATION DESIGN BY
RON ROLLET

PUBLISHED BY
SEAGROVE PRESS

Printed in the United States of America

SeaGrove Press
638 Sunset Blvd
Cape May, New Jersey 08204
seagrovepress@gmail.com

Atlantus Concrete Ship

Bb

Bicycle

Castle

Dd

Dolphin

Egret

Ff

Ferry

Gg

Gull

Horseshoe Crab

Ice Cream Cone

Jj

Jetty Rocks

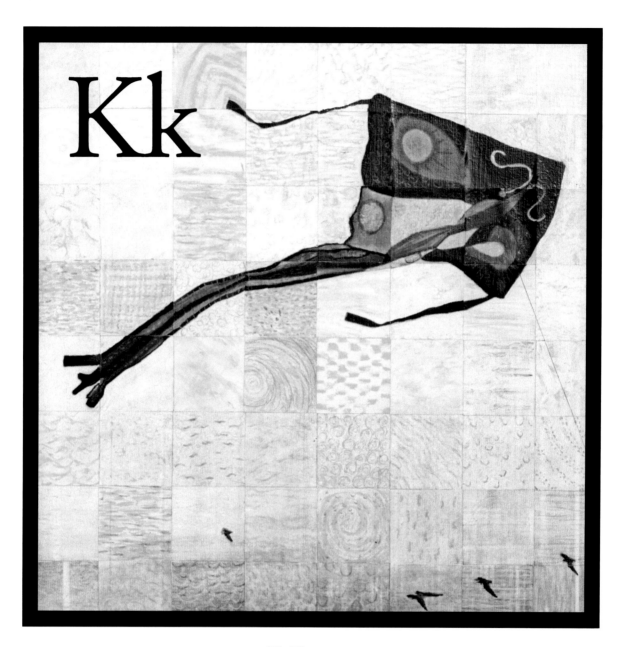

Kite

Ll

Lighthouse

Mm

Monarch Butterfly

Nocturnal Crab

Ocean

Prickly Pear Cactus

Quartz Pebbles

Raptor

Sea Treasures

Trolley

Uu

Umbrella

Victorian House Museum

World War II Tower

EXit Zero

Yacht

Zebra at the Zoo

Cape May A to Z Scavenger Hunt

- ☐ **A**tlantus - See the sunken concrete ship at Sunset Beach.
- ☐ **B**icycle - Peddle a bike around Cape Island.
- ☐ **C**astle - Build a sand castle on one of our many beaches.
- ☐ **D**olphin - Spot a dolphin jumping out of the water.
- ☐ **E**gret - Hike a nature trail and look for these white birds in the marshes.
- ☐ **F**erry - Ride the ferry across the Delaware Bay.
- ☐ **G**ull - Listen to the Laughing Gulls.
- ☐ **H**orseshoe Crab - Look for these living fossils on our beaches.
- ☐ **I**ce Cream Cone - Enjoy your favorite flavor or try a new one at our many creameries.
- ☐ **J**etty Rocks- Watch the fishermen catching fish from the jetty.
- ☐ **K**ite - Fly a kite on a windy day.
- ☐ **L**ighthouse - Climb the 199 steps to the top.
- ☐ **M**onarch Butterfly - Follow these butterflies as they fly from flower to flower.
- ☐ **N**octurnal Crab - Explore the beach at night and spy a Ghost Crab.
- ☐ **O**cean - Swim, surf or boogie board in our ocean.
- ☐ **P**rickly Pear Cactus - Search for the yellow flowers in summer and the red fruit in fall.
- ☐ **Q**uartz Pebbles - Treasure hunt for Cape May Diamonds at Sunset Beach.
- ☐ **R**aptor - Spy an Osprey on a nest high in the marsh.
- ☐ **S**ea Treasures - Collect a pail of your favorite shells and treasures.
- ☐ **T**rolley - Ride the trolley and tour Cape May.
- ☐ **U**mbrella - Count all the different colors of umbrellas on the beach.
- ☐ **V**ictorian House Museum - Tour the Emlyn Phsyick Estate and stroll our quaint Victorian town.
- ☐ **W**orld War II Tower - Look out the many windows and see the Delaware Bay.
- ☐ E**X**it Zero - Follow the Garden State Parkway to Exit 0 to arrive in Cape May.
- ☐ **Y**acht - Sail on a yacht to fish, whale watch, or take a nature tour.
- ☐ **Z**ebra - Visit the zebras at the Cape May County Zoo.

THANK YOU to everyone who came out to color! We couldn't have done this project without you.

Janet Payne
Paige Cunningham
John Safrit
Barbara Colosi
Laurie & Randy Schiffelbein
Lee & Chris Hajduk
Peter Burke
Todd Land
John Kealy
Tina Giaimo
Adelheid Helbich
Francine & Joe Nietubicz
Sister Ann Raymond
Kathleen Austin
Kay Autsin
Marie Austin
Christine Austin
Maria Metzger
Barbara Golla
Eva & Tucker Collins
Michael Martin
Andrea McVay
Betty Loper
Marguerite Chandler
Betty Campbell
Gretchen Whitman
Lu Ann Daniels
Edie Schuhl
Louise Zemaitis
Michael O'Brien
Sally Lomanno
Nicholas Zemaitis
Allison Raisch
Steven Olszewski
Diana Cutshall
Pierce Hawthorne
Justin Noggle
Donna McEntee
Barb Klotz
Taylor Sacco
Maureen Sacco
Diane Schiabor
Christine Jordan
Jasmine Bloch
Will & Colin Doliner
Shari Shoemaker
Tracy Weiss
Chloe Rama
Kristen Mains
Anne Gibboni
Melissa Cantada
Karen Verderami
Linda Kaplanovich
Stephen & Kristin Russell
Peter L., Kayla, & Patty Porter
Carol & Erin Ferguson
Maria, Jenny, Carmen, & Eduardo Jimenez
Quinn & Terry Dougherty
Dawn Brown
Debra Cheesman
Sara Mosley

AnnMarie Quinn
Penelope Cake
Virginia Leonard
Edith Joines
Peggy Kenney
Ashley & Jill Henning
Georgette Sahm
Cape May City Elementary School
Bill Stuempfig
Emelia Oleson
Beth Van Vleck
Peggy Doyle
Pam Bryan
Kyla Shannon
Madelyn Sielski
Judy Azulay
Arshad, Arman & Zaharah Zaidi
Maggie Batia
Kailey Romano
Elizabeth, Jenifer & Maddie Waldie
Julia Grossman
Laura McPherson
Eliza & Sue Lotozo
Mark S. Garland
Jeanne Shelley
Jody Swope
Ursula Friedrich
Joshua C. & Meghan V. Bergman
Barbara Hoepp
Cindy Mahoney Crawford
Cindy & Evan Smilyk
Finn Duffy
Janet McShain
Stephen Avvento
Ian Ward
Arthur Spackman
Elizabeth B.
Julie Hopp
Beth Dowdcell
Christopher Ball
Kristin Russell
Patty Porter
Rachel Palermo
Joseph Stocke
Donna Tomlin
Libby Hall
Bill & Cathy Eppright
Deedie McMahon
Gloria Cucinello
Quinn Bethell
Jennie Kirsch
Anna O'Connor
Valerie Driscoll
Anita Roth
Karin Goldmark
Claire Lomax
Lenna Mele
Amy Graziani
Stephanie Graziani-Newburger
Aidan Lowe
Christopher Gieda
Jan Dwyer
Joe Reilly
Nicole Smith
Kate Krawczuk

Bella Cirrinicioni
Rebecca Allmond
Jeffrey H. Arfer
MaryAnn Hutchinson
Irene & Nicholas Valiante
Kathleen Shaw
Victoria Benefield
Mary Helmken
Marge Dysart
Susan & Andi Witham
Patricia Grove
Persa & Rich Tomisso
Rowan & Fran Garretson
Kaylee Monohon
Stephanie Hollis
Shay Johnson
Maria Polito
Sheila Rose
Joe Capistinn
Debbie Wer
Julianna
Trish & Mia Owiskey
Mary Ann Mulzet
Genevieve McCaney
Jeanne Degatano
Patricia Neville
Barbara A. Taylor
Maureen Kolakuwski
Pam Juni
Peggy Arnold
Esther Grassi
Joan McCann
Ann Gairo
Sharyne Albertson
Mary Stewart
Denise Adams
Hannah & Kaitlyn Iannone
Holly Turner
Maya & Ron Wenger
Xavier Freeman
Tessa
Kaitlyn
Don & Caitlin Bonifacio
Aylin Alvarez
Layla Nunez
Cara
Olivia Miller
Jay Gurdgiel
Krysta & Thomas Eisiminger
Savannah & Alexandra Bruno
Georgette Morrison
Brendan Shafer
Gavin Knocke
Dempsey
Jayci Shivers
Nicholas Chase
Linda Burgin
Emma Moody
Isabelle Bennett
Mary Maleski
Grace, Shane, & Mark McLaughlin
Trudy & Aiden Grogan
Megan Crewe
Ron Rollet
Kim Hannum
Linda Horner

Mildred Morgan
Patricia Roberts
Patrice Callahan
Ashley Fowler
Kristina Stump
Patricia Allen
Cathie Williamson
Martha M. Maczko
Aviva Spetgang
Christina Davis
Jude Brown
Lee Ann Puleo
Christine Peck
Barbara McPherson
Suzie & Victoria Sambenedetto
Joseph Martino
Erin Finn
Ray Saraceni
Barbara Place
Gina Reo
Tara O'Connor
Carol Esterman
Roxane Scherer
Andrea Pefeso
Lynne Evans
Ginny Yulich
Theresa Boyce
Mims Gross
Kirsten Gross
Alicia Fuksova
Ladislav Fuks
Rosemarie Horner
Cindy Kirby
Adlai & Freya Bohn
Michael, Sage, Hudson, Aria Boschen & Nicole Pense
Amanda Leipert
Carolyn MacMullen
Susan McMahon
Lori Fernandi
Dennis Frisco
Lisa Vanloan
Mike DeMusz
JoAnne Long
Barbara Pope
Gail G. Fitz
Mary Lynch-Chory
Judy Love
Ron Goldstein
Becky Carvillano
Michelle Uhl
Dennis Foster
Betsy Schiffbauer
Victoria Manor Nursing Home Residents:
  Kathy Martin
  Helen Morin
  Barbara Dvorak
  Mary Norton
  DJ Petit
  Carolyn Reeves
  Harry Bruner
  Helen Pike
  Fran Robinette
  Betty Cornely
Alison Bjork
Roseann Baker

Bonnie Pontin
Diane Friedrich
Kate Dillon
Marie Dickson
Abigail Prikockis
Jami Darling-Chandler
Donna Aubinoe
Earle McCartney
Lee Shupert
Marilyn Franey
Kym LaGattuta
Bridgett Bates
Kari Miller
Susan DuBois
Juliana Pash
Olivia & Maxwell Friedman
Donna Mallon
Don Leary
Zhanna Medyakova
Patricia Gonzalez
Kim & Catie Boylan
Maria Lopez
Layla & Sarai van Hest
Jaelyn Johnson
Hilary Russell Pritchard
Terry DeMatta
Floss Roche
Renee Brill
Janet Gurdgiel
Kali Clark
Kiki Willows
Kerri Chandler
Rosemary Kalin
Lillian Beck
Jo Renshaw
Anne Daugherty Miles
Barb Sobel
Gianna Peiechaty
Mikie Souilliard

THANK YOU to the following businesses for supporting this endeavor!

Higher Grounds Cafe
Mid-Atlantic Center for the Arts & Humanities
MP Meyers Photography
Nature Center of Cape May
The UPS Store – Rio Grande
SeaGrove Press
The Mad Batter Restaurant
Whale's Tale
West Cape May Farmers Market
West End Garage

PHOTO CREDITS

Paige Cunningham
Mark Garland
Lee Hajduk
Mid-Atlantic Center for the Arts & Humanities
Michael O'Brien
Janet Payne
Skimmer Salt Marsh Safari
Spirit Catcher Photography

How did we make the book?

We ran around taking photographs, flying kites, waiting for the ferry to arrive and driving down the Garden State Parkway. We had our photos enlarged to 20" X 20" by our local UPS Store, to whom we are eternally grateful. We decided on a patchwork/mosaic approach that was very user friendly. Each photocopy was then gridded and cut into 2 1/2" squares. Each square was colored over by a member of the community using oil pastels. "Everyone can color!" became our mantra. Squares were colored by 1 year olds to 101 year olds, by families on reunions, people at the West Cape May Farmers Market, in the park and many community events. Each picture was then reassembled onto a 20" X 20" canvas. The result is *Cape May A to Z*, a book filled with illustrations as wonderful and diverse as the town and community it represents. We hope you enjoy it as much as we enjoyed creating it.

Made in the USA
Middletown, DE
10 October 2023

40531353R00020